COMMUNICATION

Other titles in this series:

COMMUNICATION

Time to Talk

Dr Barrie Hopson
and Mike Scally

MERCURY

First published in 1988 by Lifeskills Publishing Group
New Edition published in 1992 by Mercury Books
Reprinted in 1993 by Mercury Books Ltd
125A The Broadway, Didcot, Oxfordshire OX11 8AW

Typeset by Phoenix Photosetting, Chatham, Kent

Printed and bound in Great Britain by Redwood Books, Trowbridge, Wilts.

British Library Cataloguing in Publication Data is available

ISBN 1-85252-105-8

Foreword

Dear Reader,

Welcome to our series of open learning workbooks! In this brief foreword, we invite you to consider some of our beliefs:

- We do not need teachers to learn! Most of what we know in life was not learned in school, college or formal education. We can, and do, learn in a whole range of ways and we learn best when we know our own needs.

- The best way to help people is to encourage them to help themselves. Self-help and self-management avoid the dependency which blocks development and burdens ourselves and others.

- Awareness, knowledge and skills give us more options in life. Lack of any of these is a disadvantage; possession of them allows us to live fuller lives, shaping events rather than simply reacting.

- The more able and accomplished we become, the more we fill society's reservoir of talent and contribute to the common good.

The term 'lifeskill' came from work based on these beliefs which we began at Leeds University in the 1970s. Our philosophy has been widely applied in education, in industry and commerce, and in the community, inviting people to take charge of their lives and make them satisfying and rewarding.

Lifeskills have so far been available through training courses and teaching programmes. *Now* they are available in a self-help format consistent with the Lifeskills approach because *you* are in charge of your own learning. Learn at your own pace, in your own time, and apply your learning to your situation. We wish you both enjoyment and success!

Barrie Hopson

Mike Scally

November 1991

Before You Start...

This workbook has been written for people wanting to know more about personal self-development. It is about reading and doing, so we have chosen to write it as an open learning workbook.

What is open learning? Open learning is a term used to describe a study programme which is very flexibly designed so that it adapts to the needs of individual learners. Some open learning programmes involve attendance at a study centre of some kind, or contact with a tutor or mentor, but even then attendance times are flexible and suit the individual. This workbook is for you to use at home or at work and most of the activities are for you to complete alone. We sometimes suggest that it would be helpful to talk with a friend or colleague – self development is easier if there is another person with whom to talk over ideas. But this isn't essential by any means.

With this workbook you can:

- organise your study to suit your own needs

- study the material alone or with other people

- work through the book at your own pace

- start and finish just where and when you want to, although we have indicated some suggested stopping points with a ☕ symbol.

The sections marked Personal Project involve you in more than working through the text. They require you to take additional time – sometimes an evening, sometimes a week. For this reason, we are not giving clear guidelines on how long it will take you to complete this workbook, but the written part of the book will probably take you about six hours to complete.

Contents

Introduction

In the introduction to this self-help programme we shall explore what we mean by inter-personal communication. Section one looks at the purpose of communication. The other 5 sections of the programme look at the practical skills needed to communicate effectively, and offer you opportunities to identify and practise the skills you would like to develop.

Our objectives in this self-help programme are:

1. To identify the part played by face-to-face communication in our lives.
2. To identify factors that interfere with effective face-to-face communication.
3. To identify skills that contribute to effective face-to-face communication.
4. To identify speaking skills which contribute to good communication.
5. To identify the part played by non-verbal factors in one-to-one communication.
6. To identify skills needed to give and receive feedback.
7. To identify skills of negotiation and managing conflict.
8. To practise face-to-face communication skills.

What is Interpersonal Communication?

A great deal of our lives is taken up with communication. We are influenced in many ways by the communication systems we call the media – newspapers, radio and television. We also spend a considerable amount of time in contact with other people. Each of these contacts involves communication – talking, arguing, exchanging ideas, chatting, listening, giving information, voicing our opinions, our feelings, and so on. Most communication happens without individuals being very conscious of what is going on between them. If the communication is good we will probably benefit, but if it is not so good we may run into problems: we have all heard the phrases 'lack of communication' and 'communication breakdown'.

This book is called *Time to Talk* because it concentrates on *interpersonal communication*: the communication which takes place between people who are talking face to face. This sort of communicating is something each of us begins to do normally from the time we are born. We learn to speak as we learn to walk, to play, and to dress ourselves, so it's perhaps tempting to assume that our communication skills come to us as part of our natural development. Yet some people develop into very effective communicators, while others barely reach survival level.

Why are communication skills important? Without communication there would be no relationships. Sharing ideas, giving opinions, finding out what we need to know, explaining what we want, working out differences with someone else, and expressing our feelings are all examples of the kind of face-to-face communication which is essential if we are to be able to relate to and work with other people.

Good managers know that the key to effective management lies in successfully managing people and relationships, not production figures. Good communication is the corner-stone of a successful enterprise. Experts have shown that in industry people spend more time in communicating with other people than in any other activity, including production. When communication fails, production breaks down.

What happens when two people talk to each other face to face? Look carefully at the conversation taking place in the cartoon below.

We can begin to describe what is happening more clearly with a simple diagram.

SENDER	RECEIVER	PURPOSE
the person who is speaking for some reason to the . . .	who is listening for the moment to find out the . . .	the reason for the communication

In most conversations we continually move backwards and forwards between the roles of Sender and Receiver, rather like the ball in a game of tennis.

What makes a good communicator? These are the *qualities* that help us communicate effectively:

- respect – making other people feel valued and important
- honesty – coming across as genuine, not being pretentious or playing games
- empathy – trying to see things from the other person's point of view.

These qualities provide the foundation on which to build and develop the communication skills we shall explore in the rest of this programme.

Before you move on to the next section, what have you discovered so far about inter-personal or face-to-face communication? See if you can answer the questions overleaf.

Introduction

Can you list here three characteristics of face-to-face communication?

....

....

....

Now think of three examples of communication which do not involve face-to-face contact.

....

....

....

You might have said that face-to-face communication involves:

- contact with other people through conversation and discussion
- sharing ideas, opinions, information, feelings
- relating to and working with other people
- sending and receiving messages to achieve a purpose.

Your list of examples which *don't* involve face-to-face communication might include: radio, television, advertisements, application forms, telephone, letters, and so on.

What are the advantages of being able to communicate well with other people? Note down one of the general advantages we've mentioned, and then think about the personal benefits to you.

If we communicate well we can: ....

....

....

....

If I communicate well it will help me to: ....

....

....

....

Summary

Has what you have read so far helped you to identify specific personal objectives or advantages that you would like to achieve through this programme? Note them down here and use them to help you decide which parts of the programme will be most helpful to you.

By the end of this programme I would like to ....

....

....

....

....

Section One: What's It For?

The objective of this section is to identify the part played by face-to-face communication in our lives.

Think about the amount of face-to-face communication that takes place every day in our lives. Use the chart below to fill in your own personal record of a typical day. Spend about ten minutes filling in the chart. Enter details of all the contacts you had with other people which involved communication on a typical day in this last week. Yesterday will be freshest in your memory, but choose another day if this was not typical.

Communication record for .... **day.**		
People involved	**Purpose**	**Results**

Personal Record Chart

Your notes may look something like this:

Communication record for .... day.		
People involved	**Purpose**	**Results**
Me – daughter	To find out why she didn't get home by 10.00	Agreed she'll ring me next time she's late
Me – boss	To agree to most convenient day to have off next week	Agreed to take Thursday off
Me – plumber	To arrange visit Thursday morning to fix sink pipe	Agreed to come at 9.00
Me – secretary	To rearrange 2 appointments scheduled for next Thursday	Secretary made arrangements
Me – client no. 1	To discuss contract	Contract agreed
Me – client no. 2	To go through queries about contract	Queries answered
Me – kids	Tell them we'll go to Alton Towers on Thursday	Ecstatic screams
Me – ex-husband	Negotiate which of us has the kids this weekend	Fierce argument – usual problem

Personal Project

Try to observe examples of conversations between other people in the same way. Ask family members, friends or colleagues to allow you to observe them. With their agreement, keep a log of their face-to-face communications over one day. Use the chart on the next page to record these conversations, the purpose of them, and the results. At the end of the day, sit down with the people involved, show them your record and discuss what you have written. It is interesting – and sometimes surprising – to note the differences between your perception of what went on and their own. Jot down the discrepancies, and why you think they occurred, in the space below the chart.

Communication record for .... day.		
People involved	**Purpose**	**Results**

Observer's Record Chart

Any discrepancies in perception? ....

....

....

Why do you think these happened? ....

....

....

that you have recorded some detailed examples of face-to-face communication, think about the *general* purpose of communicating.

Why do people communicate? Write down at least four general reasons based on the purpose column of your lists.

1 ....

2 ....

3 ....

4 ....

Others?

....

....

People communicate for many different reasons:

- to inform
- to learn
- to co-operate
- to negotiate
- to help/support
- to find out
- to persuade
- to amuse/entertain
- to supervise/direct

Each of us spends many hours of our day communicating with others. In total, *several years* of our lives will be spent on this activity. If we communicate *well* we are likely to be successful in many things we want to achieve. If we do not communicate well we could miss out on many opportunities.

Now think about the possible results of good and bad communication. Spend about five minutes on each section, filling in as many results of good or bad communication as you can think of.

If we communicate well we will be able to: ....

....

....

....

If we communicate badly it could mean: ....

....

....

....

Personal Project

Over the next week, observe people closely until you see one example of really good communication and one example of really bad communication. Write down what the Senders and Receivers were doing in each case. A word of warning: don't watch people *too* closely. Staring at people in our culture is usually interpreted as being an example of bad communication!

An example of good communication: ....

....

....

An example of bad communication: ....

....

....

Good communicators are likely to find life more satisfying and more rewarding. In the next few pages we look at and practise the skills you need to communicate well.

Summary

Good communication brings obvious benefits. We can influence others, learn more, get more of what we want, make better relationships, settle differences, help others, and even make the world a better place!

Poor communication is likely to cause difficulties. Relationships will be poor, learning will be harder, other people will find us confusing, we will be unable to achieve our ambitions, we will be unlikely to be able to help others, we will probably find life frustrating and unfulfilling.

Section Two: Passing It On

The objective of this section is to identify factors that interfere with face-to-face communication.

Distortion

When we are listening to another person, even when we think we are concentrating, the message that we pick up is likely to be affected by a number of factors. If we pass the message on it may change substantially. This change in the message is known as *distortion*. Look at the example below.

Think back over the last week. Can you think of an example from your personal relationships of communication that has become distorted? Use the space below to describe the situation. Try to suggest reasons why the message was distorted.

The situation:

....

....

....

The message was distorted because:

....

....

....

If you have young children, you may have thought of an occasion when you were distracted during a conversation by having to attend to a child's needs. Alternatively you may have been worried or anxious about something and lost concentration; perhaps you were impatient to put your point of view, and did not listen; perhaps you simply switched off because you were bored.

Self-talk

You may also have thought of an example of an interaction with your partner, where wires have been crossed: you both thought you had a clear idea of what had been said, but both had quite different interpretations of the incident. This is something which happens all the time in all kinds of communication, particularly those which involve feelings. It is very easy to allow our own feelings to get in the way of hearing what the other person is trying to say – and of course, the other person may have similar interference operating at the same time. Add to this the fact that we do not always check out what has been said, assuming that we have been understood, and the result is a scenario of so many possible complications that it seems amazing we understand each other at all!

One of the factors which affects this sort of communication is our self-talk.

Shut your eyes for a few seconds and try not to think of anything in particular for 30 seconds or so; try to empty your mind.

You will have found (unless you are trained to make your mind a blank) that your head is full of pictures, words, sounds, snatches of sentences and sensations. This babble goes on all the time. Your brain 'talks' to you constantly about the world around you; it filters this jumble of impressions and makes sense of it in your own terms. Most of the time you are unaware of your brain's activity, but without it your thoughts would be just a rag-bag of sights, sounds and sensations with no meaning, as it was when you tried to empty your mind.

You do not react directly to situations. Your senses take everything in; then your brain picks out the things which are relevant to the situation, and what you feel about it. As a result of this self talk, you react.

The sequence of events is always:

$$\text{EVENT} \longrightarrow \text{SELF-TALK} \longrightarrow \text{REACTION}$$

Sometimes, when your self-talk is positive, it will work *for* you; but when the self-talk is negative, it will work *against* you. For example, if you tell yourself, on one of those bad days we all have, that you feel as if everything will go wrong for you, the chances are that they will. You are likely to feel negative and defensive, which means that you will look unfriendly and grumpy: it will show in your stance and your attitude, and other people's reactions to you will be negative as a result. In addition to that, you may only hear the 'bad' in what other people say. A typical example of this is a woman who buys a new dress and comes home to show it to her husband. He like it, and says so, meaning to be as complimentary as he can: he thinks the colour is just right, and that it makes her look really slim. She does not hear the compliment, but pounces on the remark about it making her look slim, and accuses him of implying that she usually looks fat. Is this kind of interchange at all familiar? We all do it at some time, whether it is about new clothes, an important piece of work, our cooking, our tidiness – the list is endless.

We can control our own self-talk, and consequently cut out this kind of distortion. Once we are aware of our own pet negative messages, we can control them.

One technique is to say **STOP**! out loud to yourself when you catch yourself being negative. Then immediately substitute a positive statement, and say it to yourself. It helps to have some positive statements at the ready. Can you think of any, to counteract your own particular negative messages to yourself? Jot them down here, and memorise them. This technique sounds a bit silly, but it really does work!

Your own familiar negative message (I): ....

....

Positive statement: ....

....

Negative message (2): ....

....

Positive statement: ....

....

Negative message (3): ....

....

Postive statement: ....

....

Can you think of any other reasons for distortion? The next task will help you to identify them.

Distortion and Gossip

Personal Project

Watch an episode of any soap opera on television. Look out for occasions when one character tells a story or passes on a piece of information to another. It may even be passed on to a third character as this type of communication network or 'gossip' is what soap operas are all about! Think about three of these occasions and use the questions below to help you make notes on them.

How does the message change when it is passed on?

1 ....

2 ....

3 ....

What reasons can you think of for the distortion of the message?

1 ....

2 ....

3 ....

Your reasons might have included some of the following points:

● Having to listen when there are distractions around can mean we miss things

● If we like the person we are more likely to listen than if we dislike them – it will make a difference *who* tells us something

● If we have to think of other things, or have other things on our mind, it is difficult to listen well

● If people are excited, tense or confused and do not speak clearly, it is more difficult to pick up the message.

Personal Project

Here is another task to work through which will help you to identify other factors which affect communication. You will need a cassette or video recorder and a blank tape for this task.

Listen to a news programme on the television or radio, and record it onto video or audio tape. Choose a shortish article from the broadcast and imagine that you are going to retell it to another person. Record your account of the story on audio tape or by writing it down. Then replay the original broadcast and compare this report with your version of the story.

Have the facts changed significantly (or in some slight detail)?

....

Write down two or three reasons that are different from the ones you gave above for the distortion of the message

....

....

....

Did your reasons include any of the following?

• Having to listen to a great deal of information can mean we pick up only part of it

• If the subject bores us we do not listen as attentively as if the subject is interesting

• If what we listen to is too technical or full of unknown words we become frustrated

• If we do not want to listen and be involved we switch off.

To get some idea of how effectively you communicate you need to involve another person in your activities. You might ask a friend, a member of your family or someone at work to act as your partner.

Now repeat the news story task with your partner. Record the news on audio or video tape. Choose an item from the news and retell it to your partner, asking him or her to write down the main facts of the story. Then compare these notes with the recording of the news. How close are they?

Circle the most appropriate word:

My partner's checklist included	**all**	
	most	of the main facts
	some	of the story
	none	

How well do you think you performed as a Receiver in the tasks? It is likely that most of the points you listed as reasons for distortion were to do with your role as a Receiver. The tasks emphasised the importance of *good listening skills* for effective communication.

Summary

You have begun to make a list of factors which will hinder communication – a list of things to avoid. Knowing what can go wrong is the first step to identifying the factors that will *help* communication.

Before going on to the next section, try to spend some time observing people talking and listening to each other. Over the next three days, notice what people around you do which helps or hinders the messages that flow between them.

Section Three: Getting It Right

The objective of this section is to identify those factors which will help to make **face-to-face** communication more effective, i.e. the skills of Sending and Receiving interpersonal messages.

Did you remember to watch people talking and listening to each other? What did you notice? Write a few notes about what you observed in the space below:

The Role of the Sender

You have already looked at some of the factors which can interfere with good communication. The following task builds on the work you did in the previous activity to enable you to produce some guidelines for good communication.

Personal Project

Watch one or two current affairs discussion programmes or interviews on television. Concentrate on the role of the Sender (this may be the interviewer or the person who is presenting his or her case first) in the conversations you observe. It is probably easier if you focus on one aspect at a time, e.g., things which *help* sending. Then move on to watch for those things which *hinder* sending. Make a list of DOs and DON'Ts in the box below.

DOs (things which help sending)

DON'Ts (things which hinder sending)

Did your list of DOs and DON'Ts include any of the ones on the following checklists? Tick the ones which correspond to your own.

Checklists for the Sender

DOs

*Tick
here*

☐ Be clear about what you want to say. If you are not, you may confuse the Receiver by changing tack halfway through, or being sidetracked.

☐ Look at the person you are speaking to. Making eye-contact is very important when you are trying to put your point across (this is mentioned in Section Four, on body language). Looking everywhere but at the other person gives the impression that you are being evasive, or are uninterested in them – or that you are not being truthful.

☐ Speak clearly. This seems obvious, but it is easy to forget when you are concentrating on what you are saying: you may speak too quickly or mumble, so that you cannot be heard properly.

☐ Consider the feelings of the person you are speaking to. To be a good communicator, you need to try to put yourself in the Receiver's position so that he or she feels that you are talking directly to them, and so that you can make your points relevant to them.

☐ Make sure your words match your tone and body language. There is more on this in Section Four.

☐ Check that the other person has understood what you have said. For instance, summarise from time to time, or occasionally ask them questions to make sure you are hitting the mark.

☐ Vary the tone and pace at which you speak so that your voice is interesting to listen to. Talking in a monotone can send your receiver to sleep! There is more on this in Section Four.

DON'Ts

*Tick
here*

☐ Don't complicate what you are saying with too much detail or difficult language. Remember that what you are saying is new to the other person, and they need to have it simply presented so that they can follow it easily.

☐ Don't talk so much that the other person has no chance to comment or to ask questions. They need to be able to do this in order to understand what is being said, and so that they feel valued.

☐ Don't be vague: give concrete examples of what you mean.

☐ Don't put down, attack or ridicule the person to whom you are talking.

☐ If you want them to listen to what you are saying, you must show that you respect them.

☐ Don't use particular ideas that you know will irritate the other person. Once again, you must show respect for the other person's values.

☐ Don't ignore signs in the other person of confusion, resentment or disinterest. If they are confused, uninterested or resentful, they will not hear what you have to say.

☐ Don't speak in a detached, remote fashion. If you do, it will seem to the other person that what you are saying is uninteresting, or not to do with them.

☐ Don't pretend or exaggerate. If you do this, you will devalue what you are trying to communicate. It is also very annoying for the other person!

Looking at the list of DOs and DON'Ts for the Sender, are there any of which you know you are guilty, and would like to make a note of and work on? Just being aware of them will help you to counteract them. Jot down, in the space given, *one* thing to watch out for, and *one* thing which you know you do well.

I will watch out for: ....

....

I am good at: ....

....

The Role of the Receiver

Listening skills are just as important in communication as the skills of putting your point across. Listening is not the same as hearing. It is a common mistake to confuse the two: to think that if you are able to hear, you are able to listen, and do not need to develop your listening skills.

Personal Project

Do the same as you did for the role of the Sender, and watch one or two similar programmes on television. This time, concentrate on the role of the Receiver. Again, it is probably easier if you focus first on the things which seem to be helpful, and then on the things which are not helpful.

DOs
DON'Ts

Now compare your DOs and DON'Ts with the ones in the checklist below. Tick the ones which correspond to your own.

Checklists for the Receiver

DOs
Tick
here

☐ Look at the person who is speaking to you. Otherwise it looks as if you are not listening and are not interested in what they are saying.

☐ Recognise how the speaker feels about what he or she is saying. If you can put yourself in the other person's place, you will be able to understand what they mean to say.

☐ Look for points to agree with rather than to argue with. You may stop the other person in their tracks by taking issue with points and arguing.

☐ Give a quick summary of what you have heard every now and again to check out that you have heard correctly. As we have seen in Section Two, distortion can happen as a result of all manner of things.

☐ Give full attention to the person who is speaking by facing them, using nods and comments to show that you are listening. This is not just a matter of courtesy and respect for your speaker, it also encourages them to carry on.

DON'Ts
Tick
here

☐ Don't interrupt the speaker to give your views (interrupting the flow of what you are being told).

☐ Don't start thinking about something else and get distracted. The speaker will soon pick up that you are not listening, and will be discouraged. You will also lose the flow and miss what is being said.

☐ Don't let your previous experience of the person deter you. This does not mean that you shouldn't take what you know of the speaker into consideration, but you should try not to write off what is being said because of your view of the speaker – he or she might have something valid to contribute (and you may change your opinion of them).

☐ Don't let prejudices get in the way of what is being said. Keep a look out for your pre-judices: you may not always be aware of them. If you know that a particular subject is a touchy one for you, check your reactions carefully as you go.

☐ Don't be negative about, or belittle, what the person is saying. This does not mean that you shouldn't disagree with the speaker, just that you should avoid evaluative and insulting remarks. Show respect for the speaker's point of view.

☐ Don't change the subject. Obviously, this is not going to help you to hear what is being said (or what might have been said!).

☐ Don't fidget or distract the speaker. This can be extremely offputting for anyone, especially if what they are saying is difficult for them to express.

Look through this list of DOs and DON'Ts for the Receiver, and make a note in the space below of *one* thing you need to watch out for and *one* thing you do well.

I need to watch out for: ....

....

I am good at: ....

....

Summary

Do you feel more confident about your skills as a Sender or as a Receiver? People are often better at one role than the other. Think how often you have heard the comment, 'She's a good listener'. If you find that people often come to talk to you about their problems, the chances are you are skilful at listening and receiving messages. If people often come to you for advice, or opinions, or ask you to speak to other people on their behalf, you are probably skilful at sending messages. Choose which role needs working on at the moment. (If you find this difficult, perhaps you could ask a friend or colleague to say where they think your strengths lie.)

I think I am more successful at Sending/Receiving because:

....

....

I would like to develop my skill as a Sender/Receiver because:

....

....

Look back over the points in the checklist for either the Sender or the Receiver. Choose three points you think it will help you to work on.

Three steps I can take to improve my skills as a Sender/Receiver in the next week are:

....

....

....

Section Four: It's Not What You Say, but the Way That You Say It!

The objective of this section is to identify the part played by tone and general use of the voice in one-to-one communication, and to suggest ways of developing helpful techniques to improve these aspects.

The Way You Speak

How do you estimate your ability to use your voice? Do you tend to speak too quietly, or too fast? Do you vary the tone and pitch of your voice?

A few words about accent

Most people speak with an accent of some sort, either regional or national and this is regarded as acceptable and often desirable. In years gone by it was not considered to be a good thing to have an accent, and radio and television presenters had to speak 'The Queen's English' (i.e. the way the Royal Family speak). That is no longer the case, and 'The Queen's English' is regarded as just another accent. As long as you say your words clearly, and are understood, you need not worry about this.

If you can get hold of a recording machine of any kind, record yourself having a conversation with someone – or simply say a few things into the machine and play it back. If you are not used to hearing yourself on tape, it can be a shock. You can sound quite different from the way you think you do. How *do* you sound? First check with another person that the recording does represent your normal speaking voice accurately. Sometimes nervousness at being recorded can make you speak differently.

Bearing in mind what that person has said, use the following Checklist to analyse your voice, putting a tick beside the things you hear yourself doing. You will then have an idea of what you can improve on.

How Do You Speak? Checklist

*Tick
here*

☐   Do you pronounce each word distinctly?

☐   Do you speak too fast to be understood?

☐   ... or too slowly to keep people's attention?

☐   Do you run all your words together, not leaving enough time in between each one?

☐   Do you sound sincere?

☐   Do you sound too loud?

☐   ... or too soft?

☐   Does your voice sound shrill or squeaky?

☐   Does your voice sound monotonous?

☐   Does your tone convey how you feel?

How did you do? Unless you have been trained to use your voice properly, you will probably have found one or two things you could work on. Read through the following pages, paying particular attention to the areas you feel you need to improve.

Speaking clearly

Nervousness and habit are the culprits here. Your speech might be blurred as a result of clenching your jaw as you speak (this is a common nervous habit).

Tighten your jaw, with your mouth half closed, and say 'clear diction is an asset', moving your clenched jaw as little as possible. Now unclench it, relax it by moving it up and down a few times, and say the same sentence again, moving your relaxed mouth and jaw freely. Can you hear the difference?

Speed

The speed at which you talk is generally affected by what you are talking about, and how you feel about it. If you are excited, you will quicken up, and if you are bored, you will slow down. You can convey urgency and importance by speeding up, but if you speak quickly all the time, the urgency will be lost – and so will the clarity. Again, nervousness might make you gabble, so be aware when you are gabbling, and speak more slowly than feels quite comfortable. It will sound fine to your listeners.

Slow speech is also difficult to listen to. You may be pronouncing every word perfectly, but the chances are that you will send your listener to sleep. However, this is not a very common problem; most people tend to react the other way.

Tone

Your tone is a vital part of conveying your message. It can sound sincere, enthusiastic, annoyed; it can tell the listener what you think of them; it can tell the listener how you feel about what you are talking about, and affect their judgment of it.

You can make the same word mean several things. Try saying the word 'good' and make it sound:

- bored
- sarcastic
- pleased
- overjoyed
- angry
- surprised
- sincere
- hurried . . . and anything else you can think of.

The most important word to bear in mind is *appropriateness*. If your tone is appropriate to what you are saying, how you feel about it, how you feel about your listener, you are using your tone well. It is very easy to allow your voice to give you away, and convey tiredness and irritation when those things are inappropriate to the situation – or to the person you are talking to. It can be quite upsetting to be snapped at for no apparent reason, because the other person is feeling irritated about something else. It is worth watching out for this.

Volume

Speaking too quietly to be audible can be a feature of nervousness. If you tend to do this, practise speaking with your chin up, and try to 'hit' the person furthest from you. Volume control relies on good, deep, regular breathing, which often becomes quick and shallow with nerves. Always take a few deep breaths, preferably in the open air, prior to speaking – before an interview or a difficult situation, for instance.

Varying the volume of your voice, provided it is not too extreme, can add interest to what you are saying, but take care not to sound too theatrical.

Pitch

The pitch of your voice – whether it is high or deep – is often affected by nervousness, fear and tension. Your throat muscles and your vocal chords tighten, and the sound becomes squeaky or shrill.

If this happens to you, practise taking a deep breath and, as you breathe slowly out, say a few short words such as 'I want to talk.' Your voice will automatically sound better, as it is physically impossible to breathe out and keep your muscles tight at the same time.

Summary

In this section we have explored the ways in which our voices can be used, in addition to the words we use, and ways of improving our delivery.

The next section concentrates on another important aspect of communication which is not always obvious, but which is essential to be aware of.

Section Five: It's Not All Talk

The objective of this section is to identify the part played by non-verbal factors in one-to-one communication.

Normally we think that communication involves words, but this need not be so. The people in the cartoons below are *communicating without words*.

Non-verbal communication means messages passed between people in ways that don't use words. Some experts say that up to 75 per cent of what is conveyed between people is communicated without using speech.

We get non-verbal messages from a number of sources: eyes, mouths, faces, the way people sit, stand, move; where people stand or sit in relation to each other; how we hold and move our hands, arms, legs, and so on. Whether we are aware of it or not, we are picking up and giving out non-verbal signals more or less all the time. The words we use to communicate are important, but it is just as important to be aware of what non-verbal signals can tell us about other people, and others about us.

The three faces below each show very different expressions – what do you think they might mean? Write your answers in the space provided.

1 ....

2 ....

3 ....

We thought of bored, happy, sad. Perhaps you would like to draw some simple faces which show other expressions.

Whenever we communicate face to face with other people, we unconsciously notice their expressions and movements and form impressions about a person on the basis of that behaviour. Behaviour gives us clues about the person. If we learn to read these clues consciously and skilfully we can learn a good deal about other people, without any verbal communication!

Now look at some examples of the kind of behaviour which gives us non-verbal clues. In the right hand column suggest what possible meanings there might be in each clue.

Clue	Possible meaning(s)
• a person nodding his head	....
• a person shaking his head slowly/quickly	....
• a person turning her face away	....
• a person facing you but eyes down or looking away	....
• staring eyes, glaring eyes	....
• a slight smile	....
• lips tightly closed	....
• jaw dropped open	....
• a deep breath	....
• a sigh	....
• a broad smile	....
• a soft voice	....
• a loud voice	....
• a shaky voice, hesitant	....

What have you discovered from this activity about how we use our face and head to communicate with each other? Note down three points in the spaces below.

How clear is the meaning of non-verbal clues?

....

....

What do you think is the most expressive part of the body?

....

....

How do we use our eyes to communicate?

....

....

We noted these points:

• There are likely to be a variety of meanings for each clue. The head and face can communicate an enormous range of non-verbal messages. Because of this we can sometimes attach the wrong meaning to the non-verbal clues we get from other people. Assumptions made about other people can easily be wrong and we may have to check out by asking questions.

• The face is probably the most expressive area of the body, telling us a great deal about the person. The main messages it carries are probably happiness, surprise, sadness, fear, anger, disgust, contempt and interest. Eyes and mouth signal most of our feelings, and observing the face when we talk to another person is our most useful 'second channel', giving extra meaning to the words. Head nods are saying 'carry on speaking'. A rapid head nod might say hurry up and finish speaking.

• Eye contact is very important. It shows we are in contact with each other, it lets us pick up facial signals about the other person's feelings. It enables each of us to signal to the other to start or stop talking. It is especially important in the Receiver. Unless the person we are speaking to looks at us, we are likely to think they are not listening.

Now think about other ways in which we communicate with each other without words:

• body position

• clothes

• physical setting

We shall look at each of these in turn.

Body Posture

Posture can tell us a good deal about a person's feelings. The way they sit, stand, move and walk can signal whether they are relaxed, happy, dejected, tense or angry. We use our hands and arms unconsciously to give added meaning to what we say. We use them to emphasise points and to demonstrate feelings.

Personal Project

Over the next three days, look carefully at the way other people hold and move their bodies (including hands, arms and legs) when they are communicating. Stop to look at your own body positions from time to time. When you observe an example of the body positions described in the chart on the next page, tick it. In the right-hand column make notes about the message(s) you think it conveys.

Body position	Observed	Possible meaning(s)
• slumping in a chair	☐	....
• sitting upright on the edge of a chair	☐	....
• sitting leaning towards somebody	☐	....
• sitting with arms folded, legs crossed	☐	....
• sitting with hands, arms relaxed and legs slightly apart	☐	....
• hands clenched tight	☐	....
• hands open, arms reaching towards somebody	☐	....
• pacing up and down	☐	....
• shrugging shoulders	☐	....
• hands wringing	☐	....
• fiddling with keys, pencils	☐	....
• sitting still, relaxed and looking at somebody	☐	....
• leaning back on chair with hands behind head	☐	....

Clothes

What can we tell about a person from the clothes they wear? Some experts suggest that we form an impression of people within four seconds of meeting them, and that 60 per cent of that impression is based on appearance – the other 40 per cent is based on speech.

What kind of clothes do you feel comfortable in?

....

....

If you have a job, what kind of clothes do you wear at work?

....

....

What kind of clothes does your boss wear?

....

....

What kind of clothes would you wear at a job interview?

....

....

Are there any clothes that another person might wear which you would find off-putting or unfriendly? Are there any which you would find friendly?

....

....

How far are clothes a reliable guide to what a person is really like?

....

....

Clothes are likely to have different meanings in different settings. You may, for example, feel comfortable in jeans, and jeans are acceptable clothes for a visit to the pub or shops, but you probably wouldn't wear them to a job interview. Similarly, you would feel that formal evening dress was out of place in the supermarket or office.

The clothes we wear at home or at work are likely to reflect the 'uniform' of the social group to which we belong. We tend to look for and recognise this uniform in other people. We may take less notice of, or even dislike, someone who is obviously wearing a different 'uniform'.

Some experts suggest we are more likely to be successful at job interviews if we 'dress up' and wear the 'uniform' of someone in the tier above our present position.

Clothes may not be a reliable guide to what a person is actually like. They don't really tell us how punctual or efficient someone is, how caring they are, or how much money they have. You may even feel it is unfair or superficial to judge a person by the clothes they wear. But the overwhelming evidence is that what we wear and how we wear it *do* matter. Clothes that are inappropriate for the circumstances will get in the way of what we want to communicate.

Physical Setting

The way that we arrange ourselves and our furniture in the space that we occupy also conveys important non-verbal messages. Look at the illustrations below. What does the physical setting tell you about the relationship between the people in each situation?

1 ....

2 ....

3 ....

Observe people around you when they are in conversation. Is there an ideal distance or position which makes talking easy?

....

....

There are, of course, important cultural differences in the way people use physical space and organise their physical setting. In Britain, outside the home, there is generally little physical contact between people. Unless they are very friendly, a handshake is likely to be the only acceptable form of making contact.

Being too far apart or too close makes conversation difficult. The most acceptable distance in white British culture is about 2½ feet. If people stand or sit too close to each other they are likely to feel uncomfortable. Test this out by moving closer to someone you are talking to than you would normally. They will almost certainly move away.

Two people communicating around a table are likely to use these positions:

X ☐ X	X ☐ X	or X ☐ X	☐ X X X
for conversation	for competition	to eat in a restaurant	for co-operation

Physical barriers between people like desks and tables are likely to suggest separation and distance in the relationship. Being behind a desk, sitting on a higher chair, or standing over somebody can give a person a position of power. Now think about how you can apply these observations in the way you use your own space.

If someone came into your room and you wanted to make them feel uncomfortable, how could you arrange yourself and the other person to do that?

....

....

If you wanted someone to feel comfortable and welcome, how could you arrange that?

....

....

If a stranger visited your home, what might he or she be able to decide about you, just by looking around your living room?

....

....

Summary

From these activities, you will have discovered that non-verbal communication can help you in making contact with other people. You will be sending signals about yourself, whether you are aware of it or not. How you dress, sit, stand and walk will all tell other people about you, so it is important to be aware of the messages you might want to give, and how to give them. Equally, you want to make sure that you are not giving out one message with your words and another with your face and body!

As you communicate, you are likely to be able to tell from the other person's face how your message is being received; whether your ideas, views and questions are being listened to, understood, agreed with and so on. You can observe when you might need to repeat or rephrase something, when it might be better to withdraw, and what effect your spoken words are having on the listener's feelings.

As a listener or receiver, you will need to be aware of using non-verbal signals which show interest: eye contact, nodding, appropriate facial expression, turning towards the speaker, leaning forward if you are sitting down and so on.

Your body is always communicating. Remember that effective signals in talking and listening to someone are:

- facing the person
- having an open posture
- leaning towards the person
- keeping good eye contact
- being relaxed.

Now consider how you can apply what you have discovered about non-verbal communication in your day-to-day contact with other people.

Three things I can do to improve the way I communicate in things other than words are

1 ....

2 ....

3 ....

Section Six: Giving and Receiving Feedback

The objective of this section is to identify skills needed to give and receive feedback in a constructive way.

When people tell us how they feel about a job we have done, our attitude to something, or a comment we have made, this is *feedback*. Feedback is a way of learning more about ourselves and the effect our behaviour has on others. If feedback is constructive and it is given skilfully, it increases self-awareness and encourages personal development. If feedback is destructive or given in an unskilled way, it simply leaves the person receiving it feeling bad, with no concrete goals to aim for.

This does not mean to say that all constructive feedback must be positive. Negative feedback, given skilfully, can also be useful and important for our development.

Think about an occasion when you have received feedback which you found positive and helpful. Describe the situation and try to give reasons why you found it constructive.

One occasion when I received helpful feedback was:

....

....

I found it constructive because:

....

....

If your feelings about receiving feedback were positive, it is likely that the person giving it was skilful and used some of the following guidelines. See if you recognise any of them:

Guidelines for Giving Feedback

1. **Be clear about what you want to say in advance. Start with the positive.**

    Most people need encouragement, to be told when they are doing something well. When you offer feedback it helps the recipient to hear first what you appreciate in him or what he has done well.

2. **Be specific.**

    Avoid general comments which are not very useful when it comes to developing skills. If you use statements such as 'You were brilliant' or 'It was awful', pinpoint what the person did which led you to use the label. Select priority areas.

3. Refer to behaviours which can be changed.

It is not helpful to give a person feedback on something over which he has no control e.g., personal characteristics such as lack of hair, colour of skin, etc.

4. Offer alternatives.

If you do offer negative feedback, then do not simply criticise, but suggest what the person could have done differently. Turn the negative into a positive suggestion.

5. Be descriptive rather than evaluating.

Tell the person what you saw or heard and the effect it had on you, rather than merely saying something was just 'good' or 'bad'.

6. Own the feedback.

It is important that we take responsibility for the feedback we offer. Beginning the feedback with 'I' or 'In my opinion' is a way of avoiding the impression of voicing a universally agreed opinion.

7. Leave the recipient with a choice.

Skilled feedback offers people information about themselves in a way which leaves them with a choice of whether to act on it or not.

8. Think what it says about you.

Feedback is likely to say as much about the giver as the receiver. It will say a good deal about our values and what we focus on in others.

9. Give the feedback as soon as you can after the event.

Otherwise our comments will not be as relevant. The event may have been superseded by something which makes our original feedback meaningless.

All of us are in the position of giving feedback to another person more frequently than we may at first imagine. It may be to a child, a partner or a friend in our home life, or to a colleague or contact at work.

Think about one occasion when you gave feedback to a person recently. Was the situation at home, at work, somewhere else?

....

What was your relationship to the person?

....

After reading through the guidelines above, do you feel the feedback you gave was constructive?

....

Which points do you feel you could work to improve on in future?

....

....

....

If we are on the receiving end of feedback, we can help ourselves by encouraging the giver to use some of the above skills. We can also help ourselves by following these guidelines.

Guidelines for Receiving Feedback

1. **Listen to the feedback rather than immediately rejecting it or arguing with it.**

    Feedback can be uncomfortable to receive, but we may be at a disadvantage if we do not hear what people think. However, remember that you are entitled to your opinion and you may choose to ignore feedback if you feel it is irrelevant.

2. **Be clear about what is being said.**

    Make sure you understand the feedback or you may not be able to use it fully. Avoid jumping to conclusions or immediately becoming defensive.

3. **Check it out with others rather than relying on only one source.**

    If we rely on only one source of feedback, then we may imagine that the individual's opinion is shared by everybody. We may find that other people view us differently and this can keep the feedback in proportion.

4. **Ask for the feedback you want but don't get.**

    We may have to ask for feedback if we do not come by it naturally. Sometimes the feedback we get may be restricted to one aspect of our behaviour and we may have to request feedback which we would find useful but do not get.

5. **Decide what you will do as a result of the feedback.**

    We can use feedback to help our own development. When we receive it, we can assess its value, the consequences of ignoring it or using it, and finally decide what we will do as a result of it.

    Finally, thank the person for giving the feedback. We might benefit from it and it may not have been easy for the person to give.

Now consider the above suggestions for receiving feedback – could you work on one or two of them to improve the feedback you get? Are any of them particularly relevant to your situation or to your behaviour when receiving feedback? Use the space below to write down what action you intend to take:

The area I intend to work on when receiving feedback is: ....

....

....

Summary

Giving and receiving feedback is not easy, and nobody enjoys either situation. Following these guidelines will make it easier, and prevent it developing into a conflict situation.

The next section deals with the subject of conflict, and how to manage it.

Section Seven: Discussions and Arguments; Managing Conflict

It is often difficult to tell the difference between a discussion and an argument – sometimes it is to do with our perception: the person putting their case may see it as a discussion while the other person sees it as an argument. All too often a situation will turn into one of conflict as one person loses control of the situation, followed by the other.

This section introduces five negotiating skills for managing conflict in our daily lives. These are basic skills of communication and assertiveness, and need to be developed and practised. The exercising of any kind of skill is a deliberate process. Clear thinking plays a vital part; emotional involvement is less important as you can't think clearly in a rush of self-pity or anger.

This does not necessarily mean that, having completed this section of the book, you will be able to manage any conflict situation, nor that you will suddenly be capable of keeping calm in any circumstance!

It is as well to be aware that, even if we are adept at using them, these skills may *not* work because:

● it takes two to resolve a conflict

● people may not respond to what is basically assertive behaviour with assertive behaviour themselves. Someone who chooses to respond passively or aggressively opts out of the problem solving process, and you are on your own.

Having a basic knowledge of conflict management skills will give you more of a chance more of the time, and leave you feeling that you did your best.

How Do You Feel About Conflict?

Jot down in the box below all the words which describe how you feel about conflict. Do it quickly, without thinking too much.

The way you feel about conflict has a direct bearing on the way you instinctively handle it. Do you keep your head when you are under pressure, or under attack? Are you a sulker or an exploder or a negotiator? Do you simmer, blow, or run away? It helps to know our own behaviour patterns, so that we can modify our reactions in order to put our case better.

Jot down now in the box below any words that come to mind as you think of yourself in a contentious situation.

Now check this out with someone who knows you well – your partner or a member of your family. They may be able to add a few more words to the list!

What Are the Causes of Conflict?

Conflict can be classified by looking at the causes of it.

Conflict is a difference of

Interests

A row between a customer and a shopkeeper about how much change should be given may be a conflict of *interests*: a difference between what each of them wants out of the transaction.

Understanding

I think you are quiet because you are sulking, but actually you are being quiet because you feel ill. This is a conflict of *understanding* because there is a difference between what you understand and what I understand.

Values

An argument between two people about whether to give money to a tramp who will probably spend it on drink is a conflict of *values*: it is important to one arguer to give to people less fortunate than ourselves as a matter of principle, and to the other that we should not help other people to poison themselves with alcohol.

Style

Conflict caused by one person wanting to do the shopping slowly and methodically, with a list and plenty of time to spare, and the other person wanting to do it quickly and at the last minute, in order to waste as little time as possible on it, is one of *style*.

Opinion

I think game shows on the television are good entertainment, and you think that they are boring and in dreadful taste. This is a conflict of *opinion*.

Conflict Log

Think of three conflict situations that you have either been directly involved in, or have observed recently. Write down the situation, and what the conflict was about. Then try to classify the cause of conflict in the terms outlined above (interests, understanding, values, style, opinion). It is a good deal easier if you can choose simple conflict situations pivoting on one issue per situation.

Situation 1: ....

....

The issue: ....

....

The cause of conflict: ....

Situation 2: ....

....

The issue: ....

....

The cause of conflict: ....

Situation 3: ....

....

The issue: ....

....

The cause of conflict: ....

The Five Skills of Negotiation

There are three basic ways of dealing with conflict:

> aggressively – fight it
> passively – duck it
> assertively – negotiate it.

Look at the words you used at the beginning of this section, about conflict and about your behaviour in a conflict situation. Which of the ways listed above do you think is generally your style?

If yours is instinctively the 'negotiate it' style of behaviour, then you will find developing negotiating skills relatively easy. However, most of us tend to behave either passively or aggressively, which means that we have to work a little harder for a win/win resolution!

The skills are:

1. Spot It!

If you don't spot a conflict situation early enough, it becomes harder to manage. Spotting conflict is not as easy as it sounds, partly because it is sometimes the result of poor communication and misunderstanding which is not obvious at first. Secondly, a situation can escalate very quickly once we are caught up in it. Perhaps we have been too involved to notice when it started – or (for those of us who tend to be aggressive) perhaps we simply didn't want to stop!

Write down under the headings below some of the verbal and non-verbal behaviour which might provoke conflict.

VERBAL	NON-VERBAL
(the way words are used)	(the way actions are used)

....

....

....

....

....

We thought of:

Verbal behaviour: insults, sarcasm, slow emphasis, complaint, challenge, refusal, denial, shouting.

Non-verbal behaviour: door slamming, sighing, laughing inappropriately, violence, going very quiet, growing restless and agitated, leaving the room.

You may have thought of many more things – there are all sorts of inventive ways that people will use to provoke someone else.

Once you have spotted conflict approaching, the next thing to do is to:

2. Understand It

Look back at the situations you listed earlier in the section, and use one of them to identify what the problem was. You have already identified the underlying cause, so pinpointing the elements will not be too difficult. There is usually more than one point of conflict in any situation. To be able to resolve it, we need to develop the skill of understanding the other person's point of view.

What are the different points of view in the situation you have chosen?

First person's points of view:

1 ....

2 ....

3 ....

Second person's points of view:

1 ....

2 ....

3 ....

3. Look for a Win/Win Solution

Being sensitive to conflict clues, and understanding the other person's point of view is important, but choosing the appropriate way to manage it is crucial. You can decide on one of three strategies. You can decide to:

- do something and look for the win/win; there is a win/win solution to most conflicts.
- do something and end up with a win/lose solution, where someone ends up having 'lost'.
- do nothing. Sometimes this is appropriate, and the situation resolves itself. However, it is as well to double check with yourself that you haven't just ducked the issue.

The ultimate aim of negotiation is to settle an argument leaving everybody feeling that they have won – or, less idealistically, leaving nobody feeling that they have lost out.

Using one of the situations you chose earlier, can you think of three different outcomes, based on the three ways of dealing with it?

Win/win: ....

....

Win/lose: ....

....

Do nothing: ....

....

Once you have decided on the way you will deal with it, you will need to:

4. Act at the Right Time

The key to this skill is to stand back long enough to answer three important questions. You need to ask yourself:

- Does this matter enough to me?
- Do I have time to act on it?
- Is this the right time to act?

Finding a win/win solution requires cool thinking, collaboration and calm.

The best time to act, of course, is before the conflict begins, which is why you need to develop the first skill of spotting it. However, once you are in the situation you will need to keep control of your emotions to be able to think clearly. Trying to see the other person's point of view can sometimes keep your mind off your own emotions, and gives you time to ask the appropriate questions.

5. Check It Out

When you have used the last four skills, and you have managed to reach a win/win resolution, it is important to check it out, either by going over the ground again yourself or by asking the other person involved whether they felt comfortable with the solution.

Personal Project

Use the questionnaire on the next two pages to check out and analyse your skills in the next conflict situation you find yourself in. By doing this, you will be able to pinpoint the areas you need to work on.

The Check It Out Questionnaire

1.	**When was your conflict?**
2.	**Who was it with?**
3.	**What was it about?** (Describe the argument briefly)
4.	**Causes** Was the conflict because of a difference of: a) **Interests** (the difference between what you wanted and what he/she wanted)
	b) **Understanding** (the difference between what you understood and what he/she understood)
	c) **Values** (the difference between what's important to you and what's important to him/her)
	d) **Style** (the difference between the way you do things and the way he/she does things)
	e) **Opinion** (the difference between what you think and what he/she thinks)
	Tick the appropriate box and note down briefly the actual cause, e.g: d) Sue likes to dress in brilliant colours, lots of make-up, etc. I hate the way this draws attention to us.
5.	**Style of response** How did you react? Did you: a) Feel angry and show it?
	b) Feel angry but were afraid to show it?
	c) Feel angry but realise you would have to talk calmly about it?
6.	**Is this your normal reaction to conflict?**

7. Did this style of response leave you feeling good:
a) About yourself?

b) About the other person?

8. Negotiating the conflict
When you spotted the conflict, what did you actually *say* to the other person?

9.
a) Did you understand clearly what the other person's point of view was?

b) If not, what did you do to find out?

c) If 'nothing', why?

10. Did you:
a) Want to win the argument and beat the other person?

b) Know that you would lose, so there was no point trying?

c) Look for a way where there were no losers?

11. Did you:
a) Jump straight in with your response?

b) Pause to think before speaking?

c) Let too much time go by before making your reply?

12.
a) Did you feel good/bad at the end of the conflict? Describe your mood.

b) Did the other person feel good/bad at the finish?
Describe what you think was his/her mood.

13. Who won?
a) You?

b) Him/her?

c) Both of you?

Summary

In this section you have been introduced to the skills of negotiation:

- Spot it
- Understand it
- Look for the win/win
- Act at the right time
- Check it out.

When you have checked out your next conflict situation using the questionnaire, you will know where your weak points are, and you will be able to work on them.

I need to work on: ....

....

....

Section Eight: Making Contact

The objective of this section is to practise face-to-face communication skills.

Communication involves contact with other people. Becoming skilful at communicating requires opportunities to practise the skills we have looked at with other people. This section suggests activities which will help you do this. Some of them you will need to do with another person; others are best done in a small group of about four to six people.

If you are using this book at work, ask your training officer to arrange some opportunities for group work. If you are studying at home, think about the opportunities you might be able to create in order to work on these activities with other people.

Option 1

Watching how other people communicate can help us to improve our own skills. Use the checklist overleaf to observe other people communicating and to practise the skills described.

SENDER

- ☐ seemed to have worked out what to say
- ☐ spoke clearly
- ☐ varied voice
- ☐ presented one idea at a time, avoided complication
- ☐ looked at the person from time to time
- ☐ gave examples, avoided vagueness
- ☐ paused to give time for questions
- ☐ summarised to help the person understand
- ☐ treated the person with respect; seemed friendly
- ☐ verbal message was same as non-verbal

RECEIVER

- ☐ kept eye contact with the speaker
- ☐ faced the person, seemed relaxed and open
- ☐ didn't interrupt
- ☐ asked relevant questions
- ☐ seemed interested
- ☐ seemed to recognise the other person's feelings
- ☐ asked for clarification if he did not understand
- ☐ was not critical, impatient or bored
- ☐ sat or stood still, did not fidget
- ☐ spoke clearly
- ☐ did not 'take over' the exchange
- ☐ summarised at the end

Personal Projects

You can use the checklist in various ways. For example:

● Watch a TV programme where two people are involved in conversation or discussion. A chat show or question and answer format such as *Question Time* is probably best. Observe the Sender and Receiver and tick off the points that you note.

● Arrange with your manager or training officer to sit in on an interview or meeting between two people at work. Use the checklist to observe the participants.

● Work with two other people. Each prepare a topic to talk on for five minutes. Each take it in turn to be:

Sender – talking about the topic
Receiver – listening carefully to what the other person has to say
Observer – using the checklist to watch and listen to the skills of Sender and Receiver.

Topics to talk about could be:

- a job I would really like
- if I won £100,000
- the best/worst things about where I live
- violence, vandalism and what could be done about them

This version may be useful if you spend a lot of your time giving instructions or directing other people. Each take turns as Sender, Receiver and Observer as above, but instead of choosing a topic, each Sender has to give very careful instructions on how to carry out a particular task, for example how to:

- wire a plug
- make a curry
- change a spark plug
- make a skirt
- find a computer file

If you prefer, choose a task at work or at home about which you often need to give instructions.

Take about ten minutes at the end of the exercise to give each other constructive feedback on what you have observed.

Option 2

This is an activity for three or four people.

Each spend three or four minutes preparing to give your views on an opinion you disagree with, e.g: capital punishment should be brought back; womens' liberation is a good thing; religion is out of date; abortion should be available on demand.

Begin with the first person, who should speak to the rest of the group for about three minutes. The second person should then *summarise* the first person's views and briefly reply, giving their own views on the subject. The second person then speaks for three minutes, giving their point of view on a different topic. The third person then summarises, replies, and so on.

When the last person has spoken, the first person should summarise what they have said and reply, giving their views.

After doing this, discuss the questions below as a group and make notes in the space provided.

How easy is it to listen accurately to what another person is saying?

....

How easy is it to listen when you have things you want to say? What might be the consequences of not listening?

....

....

Is it helpful to hear a summary of points you have made? If so, how?

....

....

How is communication in a group more difficult than between two people?

....

....

In your discussion you may have been reminded of some of the things we said on page 18 about distortion. It is easy to be distracted from listening accurately if you have other things on your mind, or are bursting to say something yourself. Summarising is a helpful way of focusing accurately on what the Sender is communicating. It gives the Sender feedback about whether the message has been understood; it helps the Receiver to listen for what is important in the message.

Communication in a group is often more difficult because at any given time the Sender is communicating with not just one but several Receivers. Groups are made up of individuals, and each individual has a different background, experiences and thoughts. In other words each carries different 'baggage'. Each person may find different meanings in the messages they receive from the Sender.

Option 3

This option offers an opportunity to think about an area that you find difficult to discuss with a particular person. It is an activity for a group of four to six people.

Working as a group, each think of at least one example of something you find difficult to talk about to someone. Here are some examples to prompt you. Add examples from your group in the space opposite.

It is difficult to talk about . . .	to . . .
being out of work	people who think the unemployed don't want to work
sex	partner
wanting a job	an employer
things that you are worried about or afraid of	someone who expects you to be strong
wanting to break off a relationship	partner, boyfriend or girlfriend
frustrations or difficulties in your job	boss or other colleagues
Your own examples:	 ....

Now as a group spend about 20 minutes discussing the examples you have chosen, using these questions to help you:

- why is this topic difficult?
- is it difficult for everybody?
- how could good communication help in the situation?
- what would be the anxieties of the Sender and Receiver?

Summary

Now that you have worked through this programme about interpersonal communication, the simplest way to summarise what you have discovered is a diagram which illustrates the model of face-to-face communication that we have been exploring.

A MODEL OF COMMUNICATION

SENDER the person wishing to 'signal' something	RELATIONSHIP	RECEIVER the person who becomes open to reception of the sender's message

has   has

OBJECTIVES OR PURPOSES – to inform – to find out – to persuade – to share – to organise – to supervise – to negotiate – to protest – to achieve – to change, etc	COMMON INTEREST INDIVIDUAL'S INDIVIDUAL'S OWN OWN INTERESTS INTERESTS	OBJECTIVES OR PURPOSES – to learn – to assess – to share – to co-operate – to comply – to negotiate – to understand, etc

uses   uses

SENDING SKILLS – verbal – non-verbal	CONTEXT time, place, sex, age and relationship of speakers, etc	RECEIVING SKILLS – verbal – non-verbal

OUTCOMES OR RESULTS common or individual objectives achieved, or compromise reached

Action Plan

Now that you have completed this self-study programme on face-to-face communication, look back over the original objectives, including those that you may have set yourself. Have you achieved them? Now that you have worked through a number of tasks to help you increase your skills at communicating, how will you apply them? Use the box below to draw up an action plan for yourself.

Two things I already do well when I communicate with other people are:

....

....

Two things I do which may hinder communication and which I shall try and avoid are:

....

....

Three things I can do to improve my effectiveness as a Sender are:

....

....

....

Three things I can do to improve my effectiveness as a Receiver are:

....

....

....

We hope that you have enjoyed working through this book. From time to time you may want to look back through the exercises, perhaps to refresh your memory and brush up on your communication skills. You won't need to do *all* the exercises again as you will have learnt a great deal already. Have fun putting your new skills into action!

Lifeskills

Personal Development Series

Other titles available in this series are:

ASSERTIVENESS:
A Positive Process

'When we are assertive, we tell people what we want or need, or would prefer. We state our preferences clearly and confidently, without being aggressive, without belittling ourselves and without putting other people down.' Most of us are capable of being assertive, aggressive or unassertive at different times. The aim of this book is to help you benefit from the positive process of being assertive as consistently as you can. *Assertiveness: A Positive Process* will:

- help you to distinguish between assertive, aggressive and unassertive behaviour

- ensure that you understand the benefits of being assertive – and the dilemmas

- introduce you to some helpful techniques for dealing with people assertively.

TRANSITIONS:
The Challenge of Change

'When a chrysalis metamorphoses into a butterfly it is a natural process, it is something that must happen for the insect to become beautiful, to fly, to mate, to realise its potential.' This is a good symbol to use about facing our own transitions, because we need to change to realise our potential. Change is essential and creates opportunities, but it often causes stress and worry. Modern life is full of changes; the list is endless. *The Challenge of Change* will:

- help you to identify the different types of transition and their patterns
- help you make sense of the confusing feelings you may experience after an upheaval
- emphasise the benefits that can come from transitions, and provide a step-by-step, comprehensive guide to managing change positively.

TIME MANAGEMENT:
Conquer the Clock

Time Management is about recognising that time is limited, setting clear priorities and objectives for yourself, and then ensuring that you achieve them. *Conquer the Clock* will:

- show you how to analyse your present use of time, including the concept of sold, maintenance and discretionary time

- help you identify the priorities in your life and rank them in order of importance

- introduce you to the many different ways and styles of managing time.

Other Mercury titles from Lifeskills are:

BUILD YOUR OWN RAINBOW
Barrie Hopson and Mike Scally

A Lifeskills Workbook for Career and Life Management

Adopted by the Open University for Work Choices, a Community Education course.

Build Your Own Rainbow is the first of a new series of Lifeskills guides. It contains 40 exercises that will help answer the questions:

- who am I?
- where am I now?
- how satisfied am I?
- what changes do I want?
- how do I make them happen?
- what if it doesn't work out?

In the process of doing this, readers will discover what is important to them about work, where their main interests lie, what their transferable skills are and which career pattern would best suit them. They will be helped to set personal and career objectives, to make action plans and to take greater charge of their lives.

12 STEPS TO SUCCESS THROUGH SERVICE
Barrie Hopson and Mike Scally

A Lifeskills Management Guide

Satisfying the customer is the single most vital factor in business success and the main priority in any business must be to win and keep the customer. This book provides a complete programme to achieve success through service in twelve crucial steps:

- decide on your core business
- know your customer
- create your wisdom
- define your moments of truth
- give good service to one another
- manage the customer's experience
- profit from complaints
- stay close to your customer
- design and market the service programme
- set service criteria
- reward service excellence
- develop the service programme.

Lifeskills is one of the leading providers of Quality Service Programmes in the English-speaking world.

POSITIVE LEADERSHIP
Mike Pegg

How to Build a Winning Team
A Lifeskills Management Guide

Good leaders have many features in common. They develop a clear vision, they inspire their people, gain commitment from them, then guide their teams to success. This sounds easy in theory, but how is it done?

This is a book written for top teams, managers, and anybody who is a leader of people. It offers a framework for leadership and teamwork, with concrete ideas which can be incorporated into the daily work plan.

If focuses on how to:

- provide positive leadership
- be a positive team member
- build a positive culture
- set a positive goal, and get commitment to reaching it
- be a positive implementer
- build a positive reputation
- get positive results
- continue to build a positive and successful team.